THE
BIDEN-HARRIS
HAGGADAH

Thank G-d!

by

Dave Cowen

THE ORDER
(finally some order again)

BARACK OBAMA'S INTRODUCTION

HILLARY CLINTON LEADS THE REMOVAL OF THE HAMETZ

DOUG EMHOFF ✡ LEADS THE YOM TOV CANDLE LIGHTING

DR. JILL BIDEN DESCRIBES THE SEDER TABLE

DR. ANTHONY FAUCI LEADS THE KADDESH

MERRICK GARLAND ✡ LEADS THE SHEHECHEYANU

MITCH MCCONNELL DOES THE URCHATZ

KAMALA HARRIS LEADS THE KARPAS

NANCY PELOSI and a CABINET MINYAN OF JEWS ✡ LEAD THE YAHATZ

BERNIE SANDERS ✡ LEADS THE AFIKOMEN

HUNTER and ASHLEY BIDEN and COLE and ELLA EMHOFF ✡ PORTRAY THE FOUR CHILDREN ASKING THE FOUR QUESTIONS

JOE BIDEN LEADS THE MAGID (AND NO ONE INTERRUPTS)

MOSES ✡ LEADS THE "IN EVERY GENERATION"

MIRIAM ✡ , CARDI B, and MEGAN THEE STALLION SING THE DAYENU

G-D LEADS THE SECOND CUP OF WINE

G-D LEADS THE RAHTZA, MOTZI-MATZO, MAROR, KORECH, and SHULCHAN OREICH

YOU DO YOUR MEAL!

BACK BY A BIT OF POPULAR DEMAND, JEWISH COMEDIANS ✡ DO POST-MEAL FESTIVITIES: TZAFUN, THIRD CUP, BAREKH, FOURTH CUP, WELCOMING OF THE PROPHET ELIJAH and THE NIRZAH

BARACK OBAMA'S INTRODUCTION

BARACK OBAMA: Well, thank G-d it's over. I'll be honest, folks, I thought it was touch-and-go there for a minute.

I mean, I believed in Joe. I made him my Vice President. Despite his gaffes. And I love Kamala. Despite nothing. She's almost as perfect as Michelle. And I trust in our American people. And especially in G-d.

Let me be clear, I knew someday Good would prevail. Because as my hero Martin Luther King once said, "The arc of the moral universe is long, but it bends toward justice."

But, wow, that was also "some weird shit," as George W. Bush, my former-enemy-but-now-pretty-much-my all-is-forgiven-best-friend, once said.

G-d made us wait forty years in the desert to get into the promised land. So it was possible G-d would make us wait another four years, even if these past four felt like forty; it wasn't going to be easy.

Look, I'll also take some responsibility, folks. This whole thing was a little bit my fault. I was kind of like Joseph to Biden's Moses in this analogy of the Passover story.

I came partly from an immigrant background and became a successful politician in America. Just like Joseph came to Egypt and became a successful advisor to the Pharaohs.

But when I was president, I also inspired a lot of people to make fun of You Know Who at my 2011 White House Correspondents Dinner. And when Joseph became an advisor, he also inspired his father Jacob to bring the Jewish people to Egypt.

Ipso facto, You Know Who started his political rise as a vendetta against me. And, ipso facto, the Jews later became slaves under the new Pharaoh.

And yet, make no mistake, folks, just like Joseph, I wouldn't take it back in a second.

Because it was all part of G-d's plan to win the future. G-d's plan also includes the coronavirus somehow and also you buying this book. So buy it!

Here's the deal, it's a sort of parody play in which the new administration leads you through the Seder services. Divide up the speaking parts amongst your Zoom or pod of guests as they come up, and you'll hopefully have a moderately good time with this politically moderate Biden administration.

HILLARY CLINTON LEADS THE REMOVAL OF THE HAMETZ

HILLARY CLINTON: Hi, everyone, I'm Hillary Clinton. I'm here to tell you that G-d has instructed us to remove all leavened bread or hametz from the house before Passover.

This seems like not a big deal. What's the worst that could happen if you just leave some hametz in the house? A little bit of rye bread in your freezer, is that so deplorable?

Well, let me tell you G-d commands us to behave as perfectly as possible. G-d wants us to gather and burn all hametz. Do a thorough job. Don't just acid wash it. Like an email. Burn it. Almost as if no one even knew the hametz or the emails ever existed.

That's the key thing it seems. If people come to your house and are, like, I can't even imagine a speck of hametz here, not even one blemish on your record, then they will trust and support you in your Passover Seder and in everything you do. Believe me, I know what happens when you leave some crumbs behind.

And so, we say the prayer for the removal of the Hametz.

<u>EVERYONE:</u>

בָּרוּךְ אַתָּה יהוה אֱלֹהֵינוּ מֶלֶךְ הָעוֹלָם, אֲשֶׁר קִדְּשָׁנוּ בְּמִצְוֹתָיו, וְצִוָּנוּ עַל בִּעוּר חָמֵץ.

Baruch atah Adonai, Eloheinu Melech ha'olam, asher kid'shanu b'mitzvotav v'tzivanu al biur hametz.

Praised Are You, Our G-d, who blesses us with mitzvot and instructs us to remove hametz.

DOUG EMHOFF ✡ LEADS THE YOM TOV CANDLE LIGHTING

DOUG EMHOFF: Hello there, I'm Doug Emhoff, the first-ever Second Gentleman in American history and also the first-ever Jewish spouse of an American Vice President.

We did it! A Jew is sorta in the White House! Well, in the neighborhood.

The Seder begins when we light the Yom Tov Candles. We do this at sundown, in order to mark a transition, from one time to another. And it is traditionally done by the woman of the house.

But what better way to show the progressive transition of our country and our religion than for me, a man, to light the candles!

I now cover my eyes, not at all because I still feel some slight, very slight, lingering subconscious shame about being the first-ever Second Gentleman, but because I will imagine in my mind's eye what this moment means for women, men, children, and everyone in our country and world.

EVERYONE:

בָּרוּךְ אַתָּה אֲדֹנָי אֱלֹהֵינוּ מֶלֶךְ
הָעוֹלָם אֲשֶׁר קִדְּשָׁנוּ בְּמִצְוֹתָיו וְצִוָּנוּ
לְהַדְלִיק נֵר שֶׁל [שַׁבָּת וְשֶׁל] יוֹם טוֹ

*Baruch atah Adonai, Eloheinu Melech ha'olam,
asher kid'shanu b'mitzvotav v'tzivanu l'hadlik ner
shel Yom Tov.*

*Praised Are You, Our G-d, who blesses us with
mitzvot and instructs us to ignite the lights of the
festival day.*

DR. JILL BIDEN DESCRIBES THE SEDER TABLE

JILL BIDEN: Doctor Jill Biden here, the new First Lady, and wow, was there a lot of work to do to put on this dinner. Joe's had a long career and I've often helped him put on social events. But when we got here, the White House was a pigsty.

I keep finding McDonald's straw wrappers all over the house. I don't have anything against McDonald's. I'll eat there every once in a while. But who still uses straws? Those poor animals.

We've traditionally placed oranges on the Seder table to represent women and LGBTQ+ people at the table. But I think we've had more than enough orange in our lives for the past four years. So instead we are going to use an apple to signify the same progressivism. Because an apple a day keeps the doctor away. The doctor being me. I am a doctor. No matter what the Republicans say. I hope the Republicans eat tons of apples to keep them away from me for a bit.

I tried to find the best utensils to make the table look as elegant as possible. But all the silver was gone! Do you think the Trumps stole it? Also, the pillows for reclining were worn ragged. It was like they never got off the couches. So I had to get new ones rush ordered from Amazon Prime. I specifically didn't buy from the MyPillow guy.

Now to the Seder Plate. First, The Zeroa, a broiled lamb shank. The only problem is our new dog, Champ, who we just got from the shelter, hasn't gotten all of his training yet, and he ran off with the bone. So we'll have to go with a meat substitute.

Next is The Betzah, a hard-boiled egg. Hm. Joe's getting up there in age. This could be bad for his cholesterol. His numbers are good but we best not take a chance. I'll tell the aides not to let him eat it.

Next on the plate is The Maror, which is bitter horseradish. I actually love this stuff. I'm going to take a hit right now. Oh yeah! That's the stuff. It really cleans out your nose.

And below that, on the right, is The Charoset. A sweet mixture of chopped nuts, fruits, and wine. I got a great recipe from Alison Roman for this one.

On the lower left is the Karpas, which is parsley or any green vegetable. Let's make sure the aides have Joe eat this one. Maybe he can have two portions.

And I almost forgot The Chazeret! I get to take another hit of that horseradish. Oh yeah! That's the stuff.

Finally, Elijah's goblet. We leave out a special glass of wine for Elijah in case he comes to announce the arrival of the Messiah. Maybe we can sit that amazing poet Amanda Gorman here. If Elijah comes, she can help him with the announcement!

DR. ANTHONY FAUCI LEADS THE KADDESH

DR. ANTHONY FAUCI: Whoa! Last year was tough. Who else needs a drink?!

Sometimes after talking to You Know Who I would go to my wine cellar and imagine drinking the whole collection.

But then I would sober up to the reality of the situation and know I had to soldier on without making a slip.

But with the vaccines going out and hope on the horizon, it's time to take a night off and celebrate with a glass of wine! Maybe even more than one glass. Maybe four! What do you say?

We lean to the left, finally, and say:

EVERYONE:

בָּרוּךְ אַתָּה ה', אֱ-לֹהֵינוּ מֶלֶךְ
הָעוֹלָם, בּוֹרֵא פְּרִי הַגָּפֶן.

Baruch atah Adonai, Eloheinu Melech ha'olam,
bo're p'ri hagafen.

Praised Are You, Our G-d, who creates the fruit of
the vine.

MERRICK GARLAND ✡ LEADS THE SHEHECHEYANU

MERRICK GARLAND: Hi, I'm Judge Merrick Garland. Also a Jew, I might add. We say the Shehecheyanu with the Kaddesh to thank G-d for allowing us to reach this point in our lives.

Because sometimes you never know where life is going to take you. A little more than four years ago, I thought I was going to be a Supreme Court Justice.

But now look at me. I'm President Biden's new Attorney General. And I'm psyched about it. G-d sustains, maintains, and enables us to reach points in our lives that we had no plan for and couldn't imagine but are still great.

RUTH BADER GINSBURG: Supreme Court Justice Notorious R.B.G. here, back from the dead, to say, couldn't G-d have maintained, sustained, and enabled me to reach January 20th, 2021!

MERRICK GARLAND: Who knows? Maybe Biden wouldn't have won if You Know Who didn't push in their Supreme Court Justice.

RUTH BADER GINSBURG: Exactly, just testing you. Let's say the prayer!

EVERYONE:

בָּרוּךְ אַתָּה יְיָ אֱלֹהֵינוּ מֶלֶךְ הָעוֹלָם שֶׁהֶחֱיָנוּ וְקִיְּמָנוּ וְהִגִּיעָנוּ לַזְּמַן הַזֶּה:

Baruch atah Adonai, Eloheinu Melech ha'olam, shehecheyanu v'ki'manu v'higi-anu laz'man hazeh.

Praised Are You, who has sustained us, maintained us, and enabled us to reach this moment in life.

MITCH MCCONNELL DOES THE URCHATZ

MITCH MCCONNELL: Wow! What a kind gesture by President Biden to invite my wife and me to this Seder.

He really is true to his word to reach across the aisle. Though I am seated pretty far away at this table!

I'm here to do the Urchatz which is the washing of the hands. We've been doing a lot of hand washing this last year. And I want to apologize for taking so long to get on board.

Sure, some could argue that me washing my hands of You Know Who finally is just an act of self-interest. To keep You Know Who from being in my party anymore now that he's down and out.

But who cares what the reason is?

Let's just enjoy washing our hands of him and say the blessing!

CHUCK SCHUMER: New Senate Majority Leader, Chuck Schumer here. Also a Jew. A note for the new Senate _Minority_ Leader. Actually, we don't say the blessing for washing hands here. Maybe that's another reason the Covid Pandemic spread so virulently, besides some of your party's disbelief in it. But we'll correct that later in the Seder.

KAMALA HARRIS LEADS THE KARPAS

KAMALA HARRIS: Thank you to the Second Gentleman and First Lady for putting on this beautiful event.

Let me tell you, I've been pretty busy, and I felt badly that I couldn't help out very much. Not that I should, I am Madam Vice President!

I think it was The Daily Show that pointed out: not only am I the first female Vice President, but I also have the extra job of running the tied-up Senate. This is going to be a lot of work!

But if anyone can handle doing both jobs for the price of one, it's A Woman!

I'm honored to describe the symbol of The Karpas, which as we all know, is when we dip a sprig of fresh parsley into some bitter, salty water.

Mamala loves its vibe and message.

Because it paradoxically combines a metaphor of tears and slavery with one of spring and rebirth.

We can all relate to that recently, right? It's like how fun Twitter is again now.

EVERYONE:

בָּרוּךְ אַתָּה ה' אֱ-לֹהֵינוּ מֶלֶךְ הָעוֹלָם בּוֹרֵא פְּרִי הָאֲדָמָה.

Baruch atah Adonai Eloheinu Melech ha`olam, bo'rei p'ri ha'adama

Praised Are You, Our G-d, who creates the fruit of the earth.

NANCY PELOSI and a CABINET MINYAN OF JEWS ✡ LEAD THE YAHATZ

NANCY PELOSI: Sorry, I'm late, I was still cleaning up my office in the Capitol. It's still a mess.

Those maniacs, you saw them, they don't seem to shower. And they spent so long in my office that, the B.O., it's terrible. I've never smelled anything so foul in my life. We had to get a military cleaning contractor in there to get the stink out.

And I also had to pick up my matching yarmulke and mask set to coordinate with my dress. Doesn't it look great?

I'm here now to break the middle matzo, a symbol of liberation. They may have broken into our Capitol and many Jews may have felt like their spirit was broken in Egypt when they were slaves. But we stayed strong and won the day. We brought our matzo and people out of trouble and into a better place!

JANET YELLEN: And now there is a minyan of Jews in Biden's administration! That's also something to celebrate!

ANTONY BLANKEN: So what if we're Globalists.

RONALD KLAIN: Yeah, what's so wrong about helping the globe?

WENDY SHERMAN: Tikkun Olam even means healing or repairing the world.

ERIC LANDER: Acts of kindness translated into policy.

ALEJANDRO MAYORKAS: Isn't that even what a Christian would want?

AVRIL HAINES: It's like saying people who love the other people of the world are bad.

ANNE NEUBERGER: There sure are a lot of us.

DAVID COHEN: Yeah, is it going to be confusing having different people at the Seder table say all these lines. Maybe the writer should cut this part?

RACHEL LEVINE: I think it's cool!

EVERYONE: Shalom to the minyan cabinet of Jews!

BERNIE SANDERS ✡ LEADS THE AFIKOMEN

BERNIE SANDERS: Bernie Sanders here. Also a Jew. Not invited to be part of the cabinet. That's OK. I'm back to do the Afikomen. Look, there's no hard feelings that you all sort of ganged up on me and screwed me out of the nomination. I might seem mad about it still, but I'm just always a little angry about something. That's just my style. I like to shout and complain. And be grumpy. The main thing is we got You Know Who out of here.

But, I'm still here to keep you moderates honest. You all need to give a piece of the "poor man's bread" to the millions of American families who are not in the 1%. I am going to sit in your Oval Office every day, Joe, in my big parka and mittens and blue mask taking selfies and making memes until you do what G-d wants and support the rest of the 99%!

Now everyone say:

EVERYONE: "This is the bread of poverty, which our ancestors ate in the land of Egypt. All who are hungry, come and eat. All who are needy, come and celebrate Passover with us. This year we are here. Next year we will be in Israel. This year we are slaves. Next year we will be free."

BERNIE SANDERS: And maybe, in four years, when I'm 83, you'll finally let me be nominated!

HUNTER and ASHLEY BIDEN and COLE and ELLA EMHOFF ✡ PORTRAY THE FOUR CHILDREN ASKING THE FOUR QUESTIONS

HUNTER BIDEN: Hunter Biden, here, to lead the Four Children.

The Wise One, The Wicked One, The Simple One, and The One Who Doesn't Even Know How To Ask A Question.

I know that, obviously, you all think I'm the Wicked Child.

And that Beau was the Wise One.

I'll never live down my past.

JOE BIDEN: No, Son, you can also be the Wise One. You can make some mistakes but still be Wise, and I'll love you all equally. That's not hyperbole.

HUNTER BIDEN: Really?

ASHLEY BIDEN: Yeah, really? He, like, almost cost you the election, Dad.

ELLA EMHOFF: The only thing worse would have been a fifth QAnon Child.

COLE EMHOFF: And we, Cole and Ella, Kamala's Jewish step-children, we were perfect angels throughout the election. Has he been as Wise as us?

JOE BIDEN: I'm serious. The fact is none of you are Wicked or Simple or Can't Ask A Question.

DR. JILL BIDEN: Though we should still go over what each Child is supposed to say. Why don't you go ahead and do that for us, Hunter?

HUNTER BIDEN: Um, I had all that info, but it was written down on my laptop. And you know what happened with that...

ELLA EMHOFF: The Wise Child asks "What are the testimonials, statutes and laws that G-d commanded of us?"

ASHLEY BIDEN: While the Wicked Child traditionally says, "What does this worship mean to you?" which implies that they are excluding themselves from the ceremony.

JOE BIDEN: Which Hunter is not doing because he's present and engaged.

DR. JILL BIDEN: Hunter, can you stop taking selfies.

HUNTER BIDEN: What's that?

Just kidding. I know that the Simple Child can only ask, "What's this?"

And that the Child Who Is Too Young To Ask doesn't even ask a question.

JOE BIDEN: Good. I love you, Son. One thing I've learned over the years is to try not to put my foot in my mouth all the time. So maybe, you know, these next four years, you could also work on that.

DR. JILL BIDEN: Your dad is clearly still working on it, too.

JOE BIDEN LEADS THE MAGID (AND NO ONE INTERRUPTS)

JOE BIDEN: Okay, folks, I guess it's time for The Magid, The Exodus Story.

It's funny, I actually identify a bit with Moses. Not, uh, you know, too much. But we both dealt with a, a stutter.

In Exodus, Moses doesn't think he's capable or able to lead the Jews out of Egypt, telling G-d: "Please, I have never been eloquent, neither in the past nor since You have spoken to Your servant, for I am slow of speech and tongue."

In the past, I didn't think it was possible that I could be President with my stutter. But I would think back to my mother who would tell me, "Joey, don't let this define you. Joey, remember who you are. Joey, you can do it."

So every time I would walk out, she would reinforce me. I know that sounds silly, but it really matters.

Anyway, sometimes during the debates with You Know Who, I didn't know if I could get a word out, or even a word in, and I thought I might lose the Presidency because of it, but G-d helped Moses and G-d helped me, too.

G-d helped all of us, I should say.

Because You Know Who was more than a bit like Pharaoh.

He just wouldn't let his office go.

Let it go, we said, let your office go.

But he wouldn't let his office go.

DONALD TRUMP: AND I STILL WON'T!

JOE BIDEN: Who let you in here, Donald?!

DONALD TRUMP: McConnell did.

KAMALA HARRIS: Mitch?! What did you do that for? We were all trying to get along and mend bridges!

MITCH MCCONNELL: He said he was going to start a new party if I didn't. You know how I am. It's all about self-interest!

JOE BIDEN: What do you want, man?

DONALD TRUMP: I want to rewrite the Exodus story my way. This time the Pharaoh stays in control.

NANCY PELOSI: That's not what happened. And it's not what's happening here either. You can forget it.

DONALD TRUMP: Who's going to stop me?

MOSES: I will.

MICHELLE OBAMA: And I will.

ALEXANDRIA OCASIO-CORTEZ: Me, too.

OPRAH: Count me in.

AMANDA GORMAN: I may be small, but you don't intimidate me.

DWAYNE "THE ROCK" JOHNSON: And don't even try me.

KANYE WEST: Even I've had enough.

MARK ZUCKERBERG: Same.

EVERYONE: You get out of here, too, Zuck!

JOE BIDEN: No, everyone stays. Donald, no matter how much we dislike you, and what you've done, you are part of our country and our story.

GEORGE SOROS: Are you sure you don't want me to get out the Jewish Space Laser and zap him out of existence?

JOE BIDEN: No, he stays. Even the Simple One is welcome. And that's not a joke.

DONALD TRUMP: So you're saying, I can still be President?

JOE BIDEN: No, man. But you can stay for the meal. Is that a fair deal?

DONALD TRUMP: Deal.

MARK ZUCKERBERG: What about me?

JOE BIDEN: You can stay, too. But we might need to regulate you like a lot more.

Now let's do the plagues paired with my executive orders.

DAM, turning the Egyptians' water into blood, but also rejoining the Paris Agreement on climate change.

TZFARDEAH, releasing frogs on them, but also ending the Muslim country entry ban.

KINIM, infecting them with lice, but also requiring people to wear masks on federal property.

DONALD TRUMP: These sound like double the plagues.

JOE BIDEN: Would you shut up, man!

DONALD TRUMP: Yeah, sure, it might be nice to not talk so much. I'm working on that in therapy. It's weird, I guess, like, I have some problems. Who knew?!

EVERYONE: EVERYONE!!!

 JOE BIDEN: AROV, sending wild beasts at them, but also examining racial profiling and changing how police enforce laws.

DEVER, diseasing their livestock, but also coordinating a federal COVID response with vaccines for all.

SH'HIN, giving them boils, but also banning discrimination based on gender identity and sexual orientation in all spheres including the military.

BARAD, thunderstorms of hail, but also stopping the construction of the Keystone oil pipeline and focusing on clean and green energy.

ARBEH, a dispersal of locusts, but also pausing student loan payments and considering a reduction in the principal.

HOSHEKH, darkness for three days, but also stopping any further wall construction and supporting DACA.

MAKAT B'KHOROT, the killing of their firstborn, but also making peace between the Democrats, Republicans, and Independents.

How about that?

EVERYONE: Love it!

MOSES ✡ LEADS THE "IN EVERY GENERATION"

MOSES: My people, you have learned another of G-d's lessons. Donald was a sick Pharaoh, ruling America like a vain, capricious, thin-skinned, small-handed, megalomaniacal, temperamentally unfit tyrant. But he's also a human being, who we should have empathy for. Just like we should have empathy for the Egyptians who enslaved us but were also killed by G-d. Let's say the "In Every Generation."

EVERYONE: Not only one enemy has risen against us, but in every generation, there are those who will rise against us. G-d promised to deliver us from those who seek to do us harm. G-d lifted us out of this situation in America with Donald Trump, as G-d did in Egypt with Pharaoh, with a mighty hand and an outstretched arm, with awesome spectacle, and miraculous signs and wonders, and G-d will help us again.

MIRIAM ✡ , CARDI B, and MEGAN THEE STALLION SING THE DAYENU

MOSES: OK. Are you all ready to sing Dayeinu with my sister Miriam?

MIRIAM: Yes! This year we have special guests. Cardi B again and now Megan Thee Stallion!

MEGAN THEE STALLION: You sure? I think this might be a little much for the kids.

CARDI B: Yeah, our song W.A.P. is pretty crazy.

MIRIAM: I'm picturing the Red Sea parting and then coming down on the Egyptians. It's time for some Wet-Ass Pharaoh!

MOSES: I think you've had too much wine.

CARDI B: No, I think we can do this. Ready, Meg?

MEGAN THEE STALLION: You know it.

MIRIAM: Kids under thirteen look for the afikomen for a few minutes!

W.A.P.
(Wet-Ass Pharaoh)

(There's some Jews in this house)
(Three's some Jews in this house)
(There's some Jews in this house)
(There's some Jews in this house)

Said G-d's got technique
Full of mystique
Wet-ass Pharaoh
God's Red Sea game on fleak
Yeah, yeah, yeah, yeah
Yeah, G-d made one Wet-Ass Pharaoh
Bring a bucket and a mop for this Wet-Ass Pharaoh
Gave us what we want, made a Wet-Ass Pharaoh
Beat their idols, judgments charged
Extra-large and extra-hard
Put this Pharaoh in his place
Smote their firstborn made them die-hard
No need to top, would've sufficed
But G-d copped their wealth, how fine
Split the sea, made it rise

This Pharaoh got wet, took a dive
Dry-land, again would have sufficed
We just say, G-d, dayenu
But. G-d. Drowned. Our. Oppressors.
And we again say that sufficed!
In the desert, like a dream
For forty years, what a scene
We don't cook, we don't clean
But let me tell you how we got this manna

Gobble it, swallow it, off the ground
Quick, eat it up 'fore there's no more of it
G-d tells us about Shabbat, would've been enough
G-d gives us Mount Sinai, would've been enough
We read God's Torah, read it well
Ask for more we wouldn't dare
But we really ain't never gotta ask G-d for a thang
G-d already made mind up 'to give us Israel

We got our Temple and our promised land
Made one Wet-Ass Pharaoh
G-d took care of us, Dayenu
Made one Wet-Ass Pharaoh

Said, G-d took care of us, Dayenu

Made one Wet-Ass Pharaoh

That's right, G-d took care of us, Dayenu

Made one Wet-Ass Pharaoh

G-D LEADS THE SECOND CUP OF WINE

G-D: Hello Seder, G-d here. You made it through 2020. L'chaim! You deserve another glass of wine!

EVERYONE:

בָּרוּךְ אַתָּה ה', אֱ-לֹהֵינוּ מֶלֶךְ הָעוֹלָם, בּוֹרֵא פְּרִי הַגָּפֶן.

Baruch atah Adonai, Eloheinu Melech ha'olam, bo're p'ri hagafen.

Praise Me, Your G-d, who has created the fruit of the vine.

G-D LEADS THE RAHTZA,
MOTZI-MATZO, MAROR, KORECH,
and SHULCHAN OREICH

G-D: The Rahtza is a second washing of your hands, which is super important with Covid. Sorry about that one guys. And another hand washing is especially important to keep in mind in the future. You can't wash your hands of all the world's problems but you can wash away some of them.

EVERYONE:

בָּרוּךְ אַתָּה ה', אֱ-לֹהֵינוּ מֶלֶךְ הָעוֹלָם, אֲשֶׁר קִדְּשָׁנוּ בְמִצְוֹתָיו, וְצִוָּנוּ עַל נְטִילַת יָדָיִם.

Baruch atah Adonai, Eloheinu Melech ha`olam,
asher kid'shanu b'mitzvotav v'tzivanu `al netilat
yadayim.

Praise G-d, who blesses us with mitzvot and kindly
suggests we wash our hands.

G-D: Fixing some of the things in the world isn't
ever going to be easy. It'll take plain, hard work.
Kind of like plain, hard matzo, hey-o! But I'm
blessing you with the ability to do it. I'm blessing
you with Motzi-Matzo.

EVERYONE:

בָּרוּךְ אַתָּה ה', אֱ-לֹהֵינוּ מֶלֶךְ
הָעוֹלָם, הַמּוֹצִיא לֶחֶם מִן
הָאָרֶץ.

Baruch atah Adonai, Eloheinu Melech ha'olam,
hamotzi lechem min ha'aretz.

We praise G-d, who helps us bring bread from the land.

בָּרוּךְ אַתָּה יְיָ, אֱלֹהֵינוּ מֶלֶךְ הָעוֹלָם,
אֲשֶׁר קִדְּשָׁנוּ בְּמִצְוֹתָיו וְצִוָּנוּ עַל
אֲכִילַת מַצָּה

Baruch atah Adonai, Eloheinu Melech ha'olam, asher kid-shanu b'mitzvotav v'tzivanu al achilat matzah.

We praise G-d, who blesses us with mitzvot and suggests that we eat matzo.

G-D: Good self-government also requires compromise, which may leave you with a bitter taste in your mouth at first, like Maror. But in the end, the rewards are sweet, like Charoset. We will now eat both together with a Korech sandwich.

EVERYONE:

בָּרוּךְ אַתָּה יי אֱלֹהֵינוּ מֶלֶךְ הָעוֹלָם,
אֲשֶׁר קִדְּשָׁנוּ בְּמִצְוֹתָיו וְצִוָּנוּ עַל
אֲכִילַת מָרוֹר

*Baruch atah Adonai, Eloheinu Melech ha'olam,
asher kid'shanu b'mitzvotav v'tzivanu al achilat
maror.*

*Praise G-d, Who Thinks There Are Bad Things
About The Right And The Left But Also Thinks
Compromise Between Us Is Possible, And Now
Let's Get To Dinner Because We're All Starving.*

G-D: Shulchan Oreich, everyone. Enjoy your meal!

YOU DO YOUR MEAL!

BACK BY A BIT OF POPULAR DEMAND, JEWISH COMEDIANS ✡ DO POST-MEAL FESTIVITIES: TZAFUN, THIRD CUP, BAREKH, FOURTH CUP, WELCOMING OF THE PROPHET ELIJAH and THE NIRZAH

(Put the kids to sleep for this definitely R-Rated finale)

JERRY SEINFELD: What's the deal with the Afikomen? The Tzafun? First of all, pick one name for it. Second of all, you hide this thing somewhere in your house, under a dirty couch cushion, in a grimy corner of the kitchen, it gets filthy, then the kids eat it? Who thought that was a good idea?

SARAH SILVERMAN: That's why I stuck ours up my you-know-what! No one will find it there.

TIFFANY HADDISH: Did anyone else have great sex at their Bat Mitzvah? I did at mine 2 years ago.

JOAN RIVERS: What do you think this is, the Catholic Church?!

CHELSEA HANDLER: Who let the dead stars in to upstage us?

RACHEL BLOOM: F-ing A. It's great to see her again. But how do you F-ing top Joan Rivers?

LENNY BRUCE: This section is getting pretty racy. Am I allowed to say my swear words here?

WOODY ALLEN: Keep it clean, Lenny.

LOUIE CK: Yeah, keep it clean, asshole!

MEL BROOKS: Who let these two guys in here?

CARL REINER: I'm in Heaven, old buddy. And G-d says Cancel Culture should have its limits.

MEL BROOKS: Really?

GILDA RADNER: Yeah. You'd be surprised. G-d's okay with everyone. No good or bad. Everyone gets into Heaven.

LARRY DAVID: Can I get some more wine down here on Earth? I haven't had a drop in, like, an hour. I swear these hosts...I brought over a nice bottle, and they haven't even opened it yet. The night's pretty much over. When are they going to open it? When people bring over nice wine, you're supposed to open it. You don't keep it for later. You don't keep it for another party. You open it that night. Otherwise, you're bottle hoarding. You're a bottle hoarder. They're bottle hoarders, I'm telling you! You know what? This is ridiculous. I'm gonna open it myself and say the blessing.

EVERYONE:

בָּרוּךְ אַתָּה ה', אֱ-לֹהֵינוּ מֶלֶךְ
הָעוֹלָם, בּוֹרֵא פְּרִי הַגָּפֶן.

Baruch atah Adonai, Eloheinu Melech ha'olam,
borei p'ri hagafen.

Praised Are You, Our G-d (Creator Of Keen Jewish
Senses Of Humor, Please Don't Let Too Many
People Reading This Haggadah Be Offended And
Write Bad Things About It, They're Just Jokes),
who has created the fruit of the vine.

BEN STILLER: Did you guys drink the third cup?
I didn't get any.

SETH ROGEN: I just had my 3rd blunt! Heh heh.

LARRY DAVID: It was a good cup, the third cup.
Pretty, pretty, pretty, pretty good cup.

SUSIE ESSMAN: For F's sake, writer, enough
with the old material from the Trump Haggadah!

CHLOE FINEMAN: He'll never get on S.N.L. mixing old material with new material unless he's really even crazier than Pete Davidson as he seems to be on his Instagram: @ davecowen

BEN STILLER: I never know when to drink the fourth cup, sometimes we do it right after the third cup, sometimes we do it during the songs, sometimes I drink it during the meal because that's what you do with food, you drink wine, sometimes it seems it never even gets drunk, it's a weird cup?

RODNEY DANGERFIELD: My doctor told me to watch my drinking. Now I drink while watching myself on FaceTime on my phone.

JERRY SEINFELD: Everything after the meal begins is a mess. No one knows what they're doing.

JON STEWART: You'd think the Biden technocrats would figure it out by now.

SETH ROGEN: Let's just refill our wine now!

GENE WILDER: How does this Rogen guy get so much work done?

JONAH HILL: Hey, what about me?

PAUL RUDD: Chill, Jonah, chill.

JONAH HILL: Me or the wine?

EVERYONE:

בָּרוּךְ אַתָּה ה', אֱ-לֹהֵינוּ מֶלֶךְ
הָעוֹלָם, בּוֹרֵא פְּרִי הַגָּפֶן.

Baruch atah Adonai, Eloheinu Melech ha'olam,
bo're p'ri hagafen.

Praised Are You, Our G-d, (Creator Of Brilliant
Jewish Legal Minds, Who Will Defend The Author
Of This Haggadah Against Lawsuits, Really

Hoping It's Covered By Parody Laws Though),
who has created the fruit of the vine.

ILANA GLAZER: It's about to get poppin' with
The Hallel. The songs. With the...Chad. Gad. Ya.

ABBI JACOBSON: These Jewesses just dropped
mushrooms. Chad-gad-YA!

ADAM SANDLER: You're gonna see one crazy
goat!

ALBERT BROOKS: Oh, please move to another
part of the table. The Chad Gadya is a very
important tradition for me, very important. I'd
really rather not sing it next to people high on
drugs. It makes me very uncomfortable.

AMY SCHUMER: Have you heard the lyrics? It
already sounds like it was written by a Mohel high
on baby penis blood.

ERIC ANDRE: Fun fact, I actually got my foreskin put back on.

CHELSEA PERETTI: Looks even worse now.

LIL DICKY/DAVE BURD: You should see mine.

JERRY STILLER: You actually get your foreskin restored in Heaven. What they say is true. So much more sensitive.

ANNE MEARA: And G-d is a much better surgeon than the Mohels.

BEN STILLER: Love to see my parents still at it!

GROUCHO MARX: I never got my foreskin back.

HARPO MARX: That's because I stole it again.

CHICO MARX: Because I stole his.

SACHA BARON COHEN: (*through an open door, Borat voice*) It is I, Elijah! Here for free wine.

JUDD APATOW: Is this your new fake character, Sacha? Tricking people into believing the Messiah is finally here? You did a second *Borat*. It was wonderful. And may have helped swing the election. But are you finally going to retire it? We still need some fresh voices in comedy. Hey, what else has this guy who wrote these Haggadahs written? Should I finally produce his screenplay?

MOSES: It's a romantic comedy about a couple that also heals the nation's divide on guns. Come on, you Hollywood Jews will love it! And the Gentiles, too.

G-D: I've seen the future. This time, I proclaim, it is going to happen!

DAVE COWEN: Sure, next year in Jerusalem!

The Biden-Harris Haggadah

Hebrew and English transliteration open-sourced and adapted from Wikipedia and Haggadot.com.

This book is parody and satire and it is not authorized or endorsed by Joe Biden or Kamala Harris, their administration, or anyone else parodied or satirized in its contents.

A portion of the profits will be donated to Jewish organizations.

Follow the author, Dave Cowen, at:

amazon.com/author/davecowen

Printed in Great Britain
by Amazon